Designed by Lev Goriachkin
Translated from the Russian by Era Mozolkova
Photographs by Dmitry Belous

The FOUNTAINS of PETRODVORETS near Leningrad

By ILYA GUREVICH

Moscow
Sovetsky Khudozhnik Publishers
1980

*The glittering diamond fountains fly
With cheerful noise up to the cloud.
Beneath them shine resplendently
Statues that seem alive.*
....
*Waterfalls from the marble bound
To form an arc of pearly fire
As they come shimmering, tumbling down.*

A. Pushkin, *Ruslan and Ludmila*

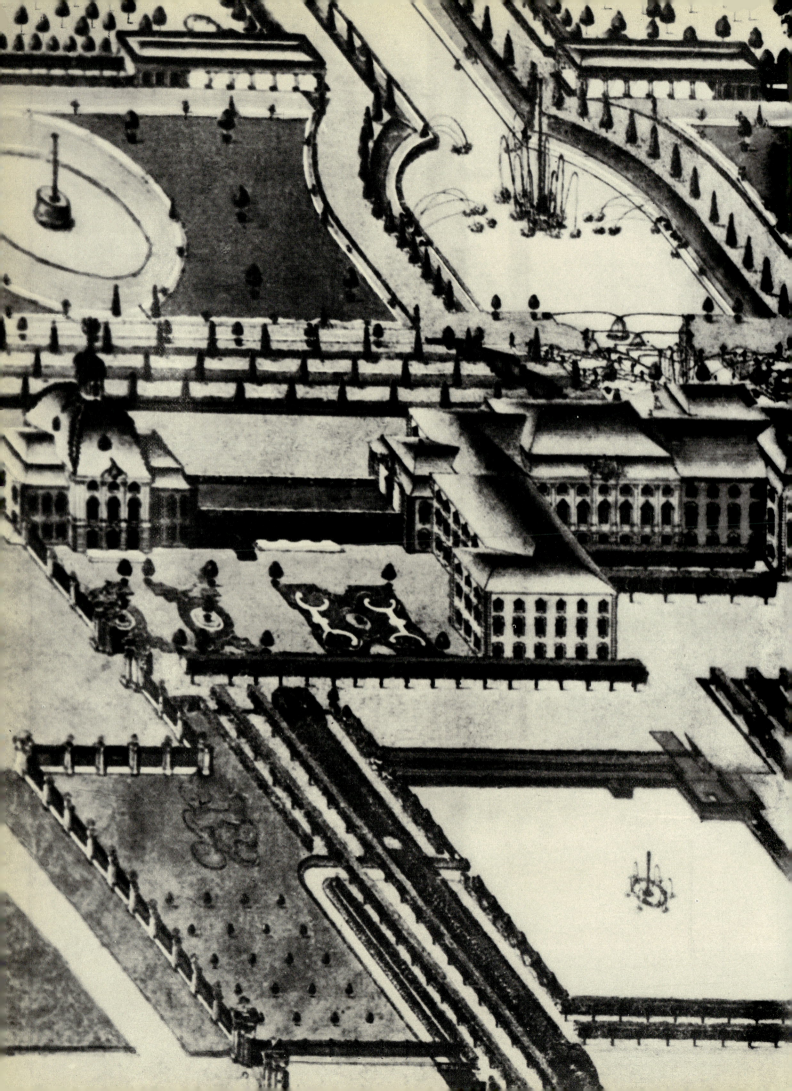

ARCHITECTURAL ENSEMBLE OF PETRODVORETS

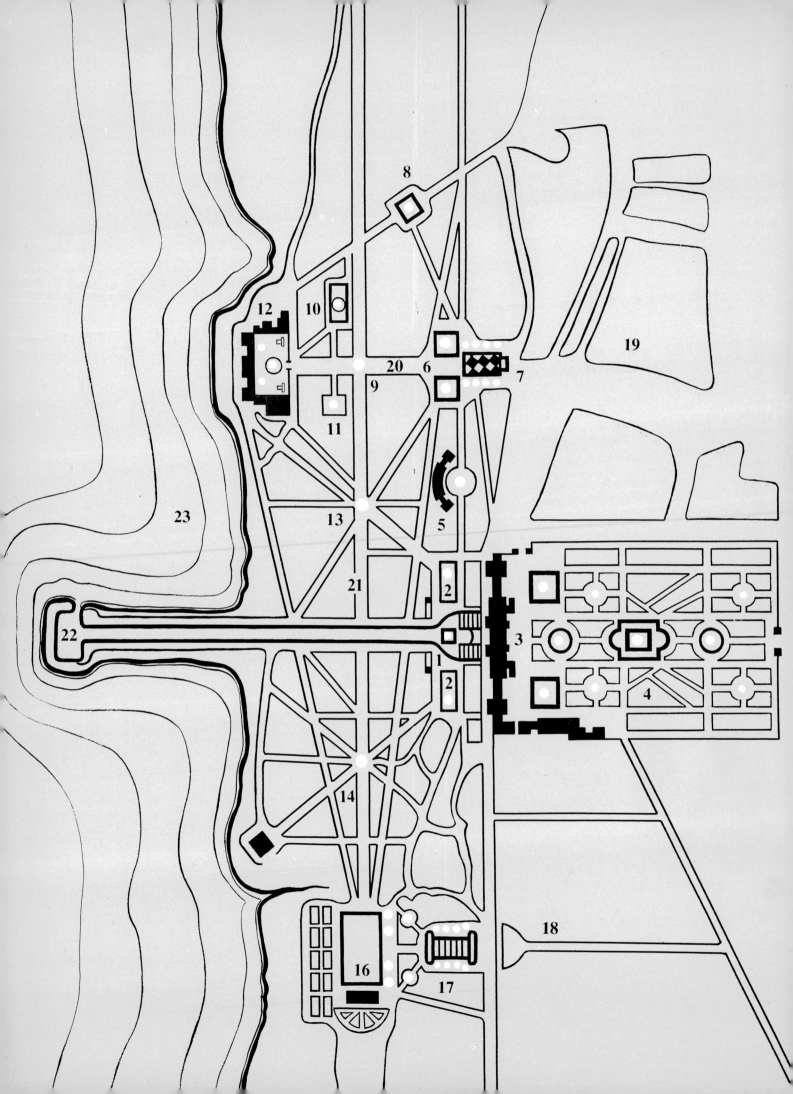

The complex of parks, palaces and fountains of Peterhof (later renamed Petrodvorets), 29 kms away from Leningrad, created in the early 18th century, is quite a unique triumphal monument to Russia's successful completion of its struggle for an exit to the Baltic Sea. The formal gardens, 144 fountains and three cascades, the gilded statues of gods and heroes of antiquity and the majestic architecture of the palaces all express the idea of the triumph of Russia "feasting on the vast seas".

Petrodvorets is a monument of enormous artistic value. It is one of the treasures of world art, a supreme achievement of civilization, an impressive example of the genius and constructive effort of the Russian people. For two centuries the palaces and parks were being shaped by many talented architects, painters, sculptors and gardeners, just as by thousands of serfs and free workmen.

The beginning of construction of Petrodvorets is dated by the year 1714.

The idea of the royal residence (the general layout of the central and eastern parts of the Lower Park; the palace, the grotto with the cascade, and the canal as a single composition) was conceived by Peter the Great. Because of the desire of the tsar to see Peterhof as a residence "befitting monarchs of first magnitude" and because of a certain resemblance between some of Peterhof's structures and those of Versailles, Peterhof was not infrequently called "the Russian Versailles". "Peterhof is often compared to Versailles," wrote the well-known artist and historian of art Alexandre Benois, "but this is through a misunderstanding." He pointed out that Peterhof's distinctive feature was the sea. Peterhof as though arose from the sea foam, it seemed to have been brought

9

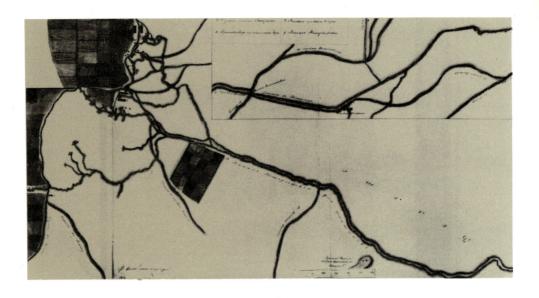

into being by the will of the powerful sea god... The fountains in Peterhof are not a petty detail but the most important thing. They are the symbol of the realm of water, of the myriads of drops of the sea swashing at the shores of Peterhof. This organic connection with the sea is, indeed, the main peculiarity of the ensemble made abundantly clear by its builders.

The sketches made personally by Peter I, the "points" of his edicts, inscriptions and marks on the drawings prove that his influence was not only felt on the general plan but sometimes determined in detail the decoration of some of the structures.

The chief executors of Peter I's instructions were architects J.-F. Braunstein, J.-B. Le Blond, N. Michetti, M. Zemtsov, P. Yeropkin, T. Usov, I. Ustinov and F. Isakov, hydraulic engineers V. Tuvolkov and P. Sualem, sculptor C. Rastrelli with his Russian pupils, and gardeners L. Garnichfeldt and A. Borisov. An enormous contribution was made by the building brigades of the Department of Building, by the gardeners, fountain-constructors, painters, carvers, and other specialists who came from all parts of Russia and were invited from foreign countries.

In 1723 the construction of the Peterhof complex of palaces and parks was in the main completed. There existed by that time almost all the planned elements of the Lower and Upper Parks, the Grand Palace and Mon Plaisir Palace had been erected, and the water works of the fountains had been constructed. The unique water conduit of Peterhof was built in 1720—21 according to the design of Russian engineer Vasily Tuvolkov.

The total length of the canals of the conduit is 49 km, and it has on its route 18 storage lakes holding over 1,300,000 cubic meters of water and occupying an area of almost 100 hectares.

The Peterhof water-supply system does not include any water towers or pumps, use being made here of the communicating vessels principle—the different levels of the ponds and the fountains.

During the two centuries of its existence Peterhof has become a most important palace-and-park complex widely known by its famous fountains, collections of works of art and decorative illuminations.

After the Great October Socialist Revolution, the royal country residence has become

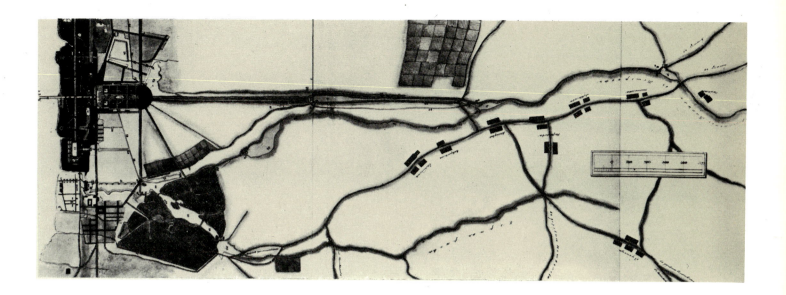

property of its real owner, the people. The parks and palaces of Peterhof have opened their doors wide to the working people. On May 18, 1918, the first group of Peterhof workers came to see the halls of the Grand Palace. Immediately after the Revolution, the Peterhof palaces were made museums. In the first ten years already (1918—28), important work was done to take stock of the museum property, to protect and restore the monuments, and new exhibits were created on the basis of a profound scientific study of the museum pieces. The ten functioning museums of Peterhof showed the evolution of Russian history, culture and art in the 18th, 19th and the early 20th centuries.

While in 1918 the palaces and parks of Peterhof were visited by only 7,000 people, in 1940 the number of visitors reached two million.

From the first days of the Great Patriotic War (1941—44) efforts were being made to save the museum treasures and to remove them to safe places. The personnel of the museums and the park workers were burying sculpture and packing and sending works of art to the rear. During the three months from the beginning of the war to the seizure of Peterhof by the nazis on September 22, 1941, 16,000 museum pieces of painting, porcelain and glass ware, furniture and tapestries were evacuated from the palaces and pavilions. The marble and part of the bronze sculpture was hidden on the territory of the Upper and Lower Parks.

From September 1941 to January 1944, the Hitlerites had plundered and carried away from Peterhof several thousands of museum exhibits. They destroyed the Grand Palace, Marly, Olga's and Pink Pavilions, and the English Palace. They also barbarously destroyed Mon Plaisir, the Hermitage, Tsarina's Pavilion and the Cottage. The nazis carried away the sculpture that remained on the cascade, including the central group, *Samson*, and cut down one-third of all greenery, including over 12,000 trees. The total damage done to the monuments of Peterhof is estimated at 560 million roubles.

Immediately after the liberation of Peterhof in 1944, the palaces and parks began to be restored by the decision of the Soviet government.

After the initial restoration work, the Lower Park was opened to visitors on July 17, 1945. In 1946—56, the lost bronze sculpture was made anew and the fountains restored.   11

On August 25, 1946 first 38 fountains were switched on, and on September 14, 1947 all fountains of the Grand Cascade and its central group, *Samson Tearing Apart the Lion's Jaws*, began operating.

The miracle did take place, the fountains and parks of Petrodvorets were raised from the ruins by the hands of the Soviet people.

The Hermitage pavilion, the Mon Plaisir Palace of Peter I, many of the halls of the Grand Palace, the three cascades and 144 fountains have come back to life in all their splendor. In 1978, the "Cottage" Pavilion in the Alexandria Park was restored. The parks of Petrodvorets, Lomonosov, Pushkin, Pavlovsk and Gatchina, forming Leningrad's green zone, are called a "pearl necklace". Petrodvorets can no doubt be regarded as one of the finest pearls.

Petrodvorets as an architectural and artistic whole includes two tracts of greenery, the Upper Garden (15 hectares) and the Lower Park (102.5 hectares).

The Upper Garden is situated above a natural slope; from the foot of the slope to the sea (0.5 km wide) lies the Lower Park. The linking element in the parks' composition is the Grand Palace, the largest building of the complex.

The author of the initial design of the palace is unknown. The first version was based on drawings made by Peter I, and the work on it was in progress from 1714 to 1716. From 1716 supervision over the construction of the palace was entrusted to the Parisian architect Jean-Baptiste Le Blond, whom Peter I invited to Russia to design buildings for the new capital, St. Petersburg.

Le Blond accentuated the splendor of the palace: he built a through main entrance hall with columns and widened the doors and windows in the central hall, decorating it with boiserie, painting and carving.

In 1719 he was succeeded by architect J.-F. Braunstein, who used Le Blond's projects of decoration of the palace. The work to decorate the study of Peter I can be regarded as most important. To adorn its walls fourteen carved oak panels were executed after designs of French sculptor Nicolas Pineau.

From 1721, supervision over the palace construction passed to the Italian architect Niccolò Michetti, who added to the palace galleries on both sides.

*View of the New Cascade
in Lower Park at Peterhof
18th century
Engraving by S. Galaktionov
from S. Shchedrin's painting*

In 1747, the palace began to be reconstructed according to a design of the outstanding Russian architect Bartolomeo Rastrelli, the reconstruction lasting several years. The composition was based on the old scheme: the central part, the adjoining galleries and the side buildings. Leaving in the main as it was the exterior of the building typical of the architectural style of the Peter I period, Rastrelli enlarged the central part of the palace by adding two wings and joining them by galleries with two side buildings—the Church and the Building under Coat of Arms.

The architect created in the palace a luxurious suite of state rooms and living rooms in Baroque, all richly adorned with gilt wood carvings, mirrors, ceiling paintings, and floors of inlaid woodwork. The painters working with Rastrelli were I.Vishniakov, the Belsky brothers, B.Tarsia, P.Ballarini, G.Valeriani, and L.Werner. The carved décor of the palace rooms was executed by Okhta carvers, and the floors were parqueted by N.Zhdanov and A.Voronitsyn. The Main Stairway, the Ballroom and the Audience Hall that survived until 1941 were most valuable monuments of Russian art of the mid-18th century.

In the 1760s and 1770s, some of the halls of the Grand Palace were refashioned in a new architectural style, Neo-classicism. The Dining Room, the Throne Room and the Chesma Hall were decorated anew. The gilded carved décor was replaced by mouldings here, the designs made by architect Yuri Felten. The Chesma Hall was adorned with twelve paintings by Philipp Hackert, showing various scenes of the victorious battle in the Chesma Bay during the Russo-Turkish War of 1767—74. Four canvases on the same subject, by the French painter Richard Peton, decorated the Throne Room.

There were created two Chinese chambers decorated with lacquered Chinese painting, designed by Jean-Baptiste Vallin de la Mothe.

In the 19th century, the eastern part of the Grand Palace was decorated under the supervision of architect Andrei Stakenschneider.

Barbarously destroyed during 1941—44, the palace is being restored according to a design of architects V.Savkov and Ye.Kazanskaya. In 1952—57, the exterior of the palace was restored and the restoration of its interior was started.

There have been finished by now the Picture Gallery, the White Dining Room, the

Throne Room, the Chesma Hall, the Audience Hall, the Oak and the Chinese Chambers, the Partridge Room, the Drawing Room, the Crown Room and the Dressing Room, as well as many others. Since the beginning of the restoration enormous and extremely complicated work has been done to remake the gilded carving, painting, inlaid floors, decorative moldings, and stoves. A collection of 368 portraits painted by Pietro Rotari and his Russian pupils, paintings by Hackert, cut-glass chandeliers,

14

decorative bronze articles, chinaware, and sets of furniture again adorn the interior of the palace. In the Throne Room, the bas-reliefs *The Return of Svyatoslav from the Danube* and *The Baptism of Olga,* executed by sculptors Mikhail Kozlovsky and Andrei Ivanov in the 1770s, have been recreated and replicas have been made of two bas-reliefs, by sculptor Ivan Prokofyev, allegorically representing Truth and Justice. The decoration of the reception halls—has been remade by Leningrad restorers.

The Grand Palace is one of the most interesting Soviet museums of art history, containing collections of Russian and Western European painting, sculpture and applied art.

From the terrace of the Grand Palace opens an inimitably beautiful panorama of the central grandiose ensemble—the Big Grotto with the cascade, the canal and the sea. The Big Grotto with the cascade, one of the greatest fountain complexes in the world, combines 64 fountains and 255 sculptures and decorations. The sea canal linking the Grand Cascade with the gulf, and the alley of 22 fountains divide the Lower Park into two parts: western and eastern. On the shore of the Gulf of Finland are located—equidistant from the sea canal—the Mon Plaisir Palace in the eastern part of the park and the imperial Hermitage Pavilion in the western. The Lower Park is one of the best specimens of formal gardens.

Three radial alleys running from the slopes to the sea, to Mon Plaisir and the Hermitage, are crossed by three transversal ones starting from the Marly Palace, at the western border of the ensemble. The middle—the main one—is called Marly Alley. On this alley stand the Adam Fountain in the eastern, and the Eve Fountain in the western parts of the park. A system of eight alleys radiating from these fountains form two stars. In the eastern part of the park is the palace of Peter I, Mon Plaisir, a unique monument of Russian architecture and art of the early 18th century. Mon Plaisir was built (from 1714 to 1723) by architects J.-F.Braunstein, J.-B.Le Blond and N.Michetti and painters Ph.Pilement, F.Vorobyov, R.Bushuev, I.Tikhanov, and others. The façades of the palace are architecturally simple and laconic, while the interior impresses by its rich and harmonious artistic decoration. Mon Plaisir contains a large collection of paintings of Dutch, Flemish and Italian artists of the 17th and the early 18th centuries.

15

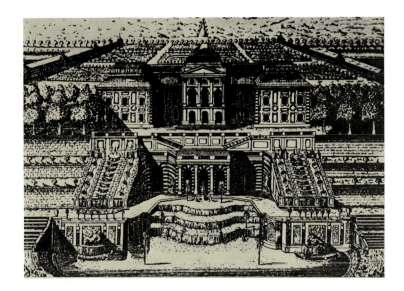

Upper Palace at Peterhof
1717
Engraving by A. Rostovtsev

Ruined during 1941—44, the palace has now been fully restored. The new lacquer-painted panels for the Lacquered Chamber of the palace were made by Palekh painters. The main decorative element of the pavilions and galleries symmetrically disposed around the central building of the palace are pictures of Dutch, Flemish and Italian masters of the 17th and 18th centuries.

Of special interest in the central hall are the painting and stucco décor of the plafond portraying characters of the Italian comedy and allegories of the seasons and the four elements. Adjoining the Central Hall from the east are the Lacquered Chamber, the Kitchen and the Pantry. On show in the Kitchen is a collection of copper kitchen utensils of the early 18th century, pewter plates of English workmanship with the trademarks of the best masters of that time, and Delft glazed earthenware, and in the Pantry a collection of fancy cut glass of Russian make dating from the first quarter of the 18th century.

From the west, the Central Hall is adjoined by three more rooms. One is the Naval Study, with a splendid view from its windows of the expanses of the Gulf of Finland. The study's panels are decorated with tiles picturing the thirteen types of sailing vessels used in the Russian navy in the 18th century. The other two are the Secretary's Room and the Bedchamber, the latter containing some of Peter I's personal belongings. In the mid-18th century already, Mon Plaisir was a whole complex of estate-type buildings. From the west and the east it had galleries added to it for the accommodation of guests, a Bath Building erected by architect Eduard Hahn in the 1860s and an Assembly Hall, the work of the famous Russian architect Mikhail Zemtsov.

The large stone Catherine building designed by Bartolomeo Rastrelli (1748) attracts attention in the western part of the complex. Restoration has now been started of its interior ravaged by a fire during 1941—44.

In front of the Mon Plaisir Palace there is a garden with flower-beds of different shapes, and fountains. A straight alley connects the Mon Plaisir ensemble with the Checkerboard Hill, the cascade in the eastern part of the park. In the same part of the park there are also original "jester" fountains: Benches, Oakling and Chinese Parasol, as well as a peculiar water obelisk, the Pyramid Fountain, and the mechanically

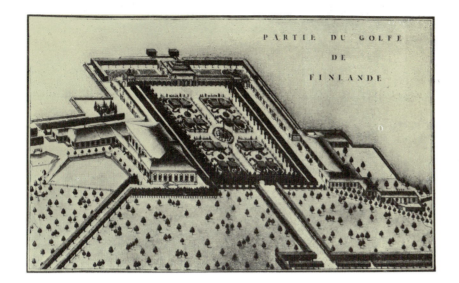

*Axonometrical layout
of Mon Plaisir ensemble
in Lower Park. 1772
Drawing by P. Saint-Hilaire*

operated Sun Fountain. Symmetrically with Mon Plaisir, in the western part of the park stands the Hermitage on the shore of the gulf, on a massive stone foundation and surrounded by a moat. The pavilion was built during 1722 and 1725 under J.-F.Braunstein's supervision. The Hermitage, one of the most interesting monuments of Russian architecture of the first quarter of the 18th century, is distinguished by lightness, by perfect proportions and architectural forms.

From the central hall of the first floor opens a magnificent view of the Gulf of Finland and Kronstadt. The walls of the hall were completely covered with pictures of Western European masters of the 17th and 18th centuries from the collection of Peter I. Destroyed during 1941—44, the Hermitage was restored and opened to visitors in 1952. The Marly Palace designed by J.-F.Braunstein was built almost simultaneously with the Hermitage, also in the western part of the park. It is situated on the bank of a rectangular pond and is the center of the western area of the park with the Golden Hill Cascade, a group of fountains (Ménagerie and Tritons) and an orchard.

During 1941—44 Marly was wracked and ruined. The façades of the palace were restored in 1954—55; at the present time complex restoration of the interior of the Marly Palace and of the western part of the Lower Park is being carried on.

Petrodvorets, a town of palaces, parks and fountains, is widely known throughout the world. Over three million people come here every year to see the monuments of Russian culture and art, to admire the unique charm and inimitable beauty of Peterhof. The revived palace-and-park ensemble of Peterhof has acquired today a new significance: it is not only a monument of history and art but also a symbol of creative power and poetic genius of the Soviet man.

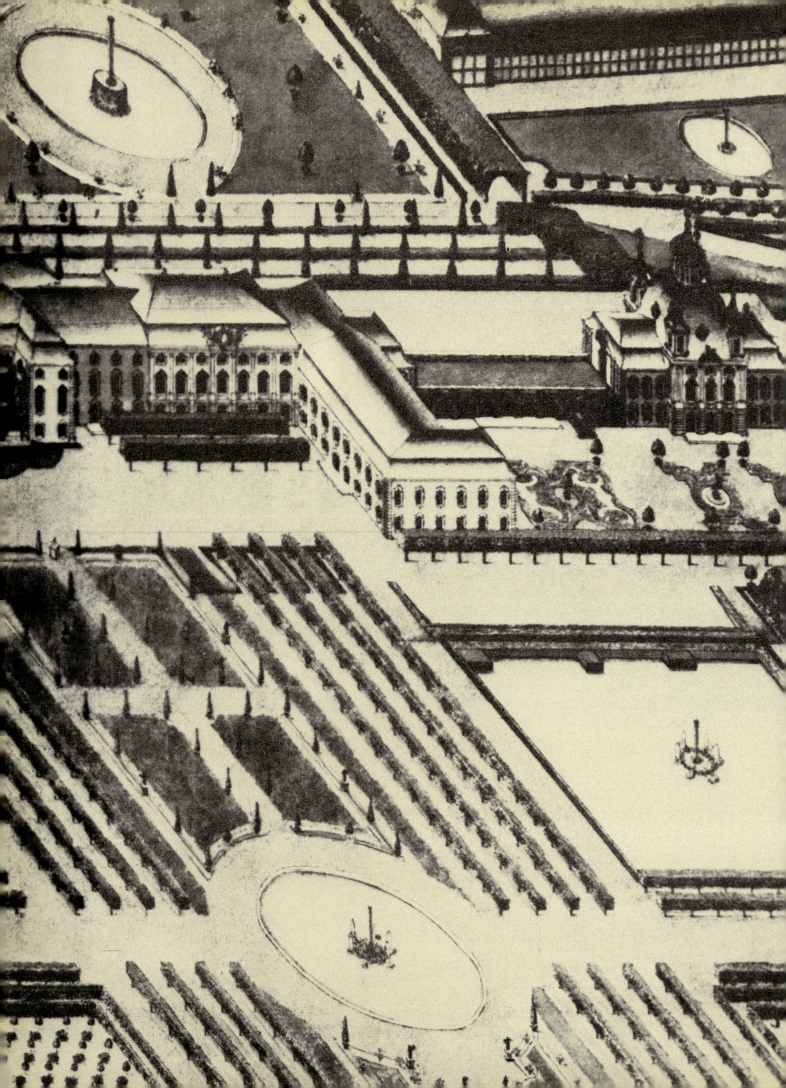

UPPER GARDEN

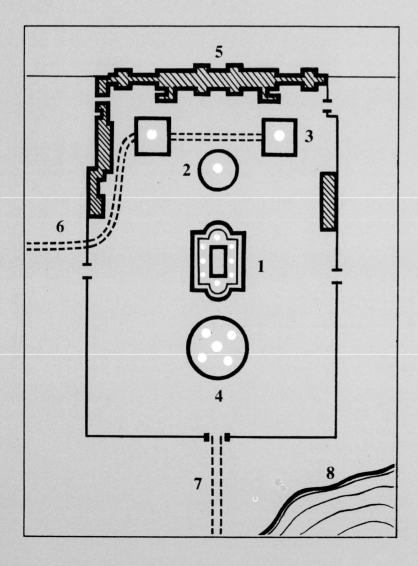

1 Neptune Fountain
2 Oak Fountain
3 Square Ponds Fountains
4 Mezheumny Fountain
5 Grand Palace
6 Upper Garden Canal
7 Samson Water Conduit
8 Olga's Pond

The heart and soul of Peterhof, of the Lower Park in particular, are, of course, fountains. The 144 fountains and three magnificent cascades now active there have won Petrodvorets world-wide fame.

Fountains have always been indispensable in a classical formal garden; they make possible to integrate and arrange its separate planning elements, to create closed perspectives, to relieve a geometrically-laid garden of certain monotony. Special significance of fountain compositions in the parks of Peterhof, which were to be a symbol of Russia's naval power, was well understood by the architects of the ensemble. In 1717 Le Blond wrote to Peter I of the need to seek water reserves to supply fountains with "playing water", for without the latter parks "look ever so dull". The French architect proposed building water elevating works, that is, following the principle used in Versailles. Though extremely beautiful, the Versailles fountains, however, have one essential shortcoming—an extremely complicated water-supply system, which allows switching them on for only two hours twice a week, whereas the Peterhof fountains today, too, work daily five months a year. Their water expenditure is expressed by quite a considerable figure—100,000 cubic meters per ten hours of work.

On the face of it, it might seem convenient to use for this purpose the inexhaustible resources of the Gulf of Finland. But the creators of the fountain water conduit followed a different way, for the use of the sea water would require a large number of additional pumping installations making water supply more expensive and complicated. This is why in 1720 Peter I himself made an exploring expedition to the environs of Peterhof, and 20 kms away from it, in the vicinity of Ropsha, on the so-called Ropsha heights, discovered large reserves of water in springs and underground sources.

21

The construction of the water conduit was entrusted to the first Russian hydraulic engineer Vasily Tuvolkov. The digging of the canal started in January 1721, and on August 8 of the same year Peter I dug himself through the last earth barrier separating the Kavasha River from the canal. Water reached the parks by 6 a.m. on the following day. It was the first day that the Peterhof fountains were playing. The official opening of the residence took place on August 15, 1723. The newly created water jets amazed the emperor's guests by their diversity and abundance of water. K.Berchgolz, one of the emperor's rétinue attending the celebration, wrote in his diary: "...especially beautiful were the fountains with their exuberance of water."

The famous Peterhof fountains have been active for over 250 years now, but the principle of their operation is so simple and original that today, too, when technology has made astounding progress, use is still made of the old system.

The supply of water to the jets does not require any pumping devices: water storing ponds situated considerably higher than the park grounds (the Pink Pavilion pond feeding the Samson conduit, for example, is 22 meters above the sea level), water reaches the fountains by gravity. The reserves of water are practically inexhaustible, so the powerful torrents of the Petrodvorets fountains will be admired by many more generations of visitors.

At 11 a.m. every day, five months a year, there is the ceremony of turning on water to the strains of *The Hymn to the Great City* from R.Glier's ballet *The Bronze Horseman*. It is a sort of a ritual, the first such event taking place on Victory Day, May 9.

Acquaintance with the fountains of Peterhof begins in the Upper Garden situated above a natural slope, while the area between the foot of the slope and the sea is occupied by the Lower Park. Laid out between the Leningrad—Oranienbaum motor road and the southern façade of the Grand Palace, the Upper Garden offers an excellent approach to visitors coming by this road. The location of the garden determined its planning in the form of an oblong rectangle equal in width to the palace façade.

The whole of the central part of the Upper Garden is occupied by a wide parterre presenting a splendid view from the monumental pylons of the main gate to the palace. The parterre is framed with rows of trees, with six rectangular boskets behind them,

25

three on each side. The garden is enclosed from three sides by a fence with massive pillars decorated with mascarons. The fence was designed by Bartolomeo Rastrelli in the mid-18th century.

The Upper Garden is a typical example of formal gardens with their characteristic geometrical design, strictly symmetrical planning, trees trimmed in various shapes, numerous trellis arbours, parterres of intricate patterns, and sculptures.

The main decoration of the Upper Garden are five fountains, whose basins are used as reservoirs of water for the Grand Cascade. Three of the Upper Garden fountains—Mezheumny, Neptune and Oak—are situated along the central alley, and two others stand in square pools in front of the wings of the Palace.

The decoration of the fountains is similar: the statue placed in the center is surrounded with a garland of arched jets spouting from the open mouths of dolphins.

The richest of them, and sculpturally most important, is the Neptune Fountain. The statue of the formidable god of the sea and around forty large figures and small details executed with great mastery form a rich sculptural parade effectively combined with the play of water. Initially the "Neptune Chariot" in the basin of the central fountain in the Upper Garden was cast in lead after the model of Carlo Rastrelli. In 1799, however, Rastrelli's decayed composition was replaced by the *Neptune* fountain group created anew in the mid-18th century in Nuremberg by sculptors Georg Schweigger and Jeremias Eisler after the model of Christoph II Ritter. In 1798 it was purchased for Peterhof. Soon a statue of Apollo Belvedere cast by V.Yekimov after a model made from the Greek original by F.Gordeev was put on the edge of the fountain's basin.

An indispensable component of a formal garden, marble sculpture, was brought Peterhof from Italy, made there by "the best local masters", The Upper Garden is decorated with four works of the well-known Italian sculptor Antonio Bonazza: *Flora*, *Zephyrus*, *Vertumnus* and *Pomona*. The first restoration of the Upper Garden was made in 1926—28, when it was cleared of the wild lilac thickets obstructing the view of the Grand Palace and thus detracting from one of the most important effects of the entire ensemble.

During 1941—44, the Upper Garden and its fountains were almost fully destroyed. In

1956—68 it was recreated on the basis of axonometric drawings made in the 1770s. The restoration of the layout, greenery, fountain basins and sculpture has recently been completed. Every day makes clearer the harmony of strict planning of the Upper Garden with the majestic width of the space enlivened with low fountains.

The Upper Garden naturally merges with the Lower Park. The middle parterre is continued in the park by the sea canal and forms together with it the main axis of the entire complex.

The designers of the unique fountain structures, just as the builders of the palaces, were largely guided by the existing landscape, the features of the ground. A characteristic fountain decoration in Peterhof were therefore cascades adorning the natural slope marking the border of the Lower Park in the south. The main element of the entire composition is the famous Grand Cascade.

Vertumnus, *in Upper Garden*
1757
Marble. Sculptor A. Bonazza.
Vertumnus, a Roman god
of orchards, personified
the changing seasons. Trying
to win the heart of Pomona,
he appeared before her in
various forms. Pomona fell
in love with Vertumnus when
he changed into a beautiful
youth. Vertumnus is depicted
with a mask, a reminder of his
transformations.

Zephyrus, *in Upper Garden*
1757
Marble. Sculptor A. Bonazza.
In Greek mythology Zephyrus
was the god of winds.

The eastern square pond
in Upper Garden
In 1737 the fountain in
this pond was adorned
with a leaden gilded group
Proserpine and Alpheus,
executed by C. Rastrelli.
In 1773, after the removal
of the sculpture,
a composition of six jets
shooting from the mouths
of dolphins was created
by architect I. Yakovlev.
Decoration of
the fountain was restored in
1968. A sculpture Apollino
is a marble copy made in
the early 19th century from
an antique original
(4th century B.C.).

LOWER
PARK

*Grand Palace
and Grand Cascade
A single architectural
complex and, artistically
and compositionally, the
center of the Peterhof
palace-and-park ensemble,
Grand Palace designed by
J.-F. Braunstein, J.-B. Le Blond,
N. Michetti and M. Zemtsov,
was built in 1714—23;
rebuilt by B. Rastrelli in
1747—54. Damaged in 1941—44;
is being restored after V. Savkov
and Ye. Kazanskaya's design.
The façades were restored
in 1952—58*

Ensemble of the Central Part of Lower Park

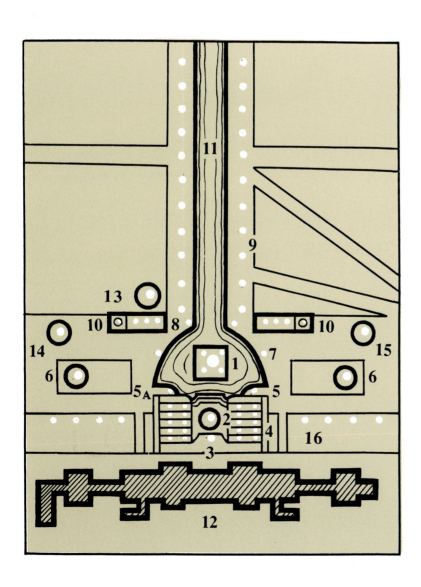

1 Samson Fountain
2 Basket Fountain
3 Tritons Fountain
4 Fountains of
   Cascade Staircases
5 Neva Fountain
5a Volkhov Fountain
6 Bowl Fountains
7 Sirens Fountains
8 Naiads Fountains
9 Fountains Alley
10 Voronikhin Colonnades
   Fountains
11 Sea Canal
12 Grand Palace
13 Favorite Fountain
14 Nymph Fountain
15 Danaid Fountain
16 Terrace Fountains

Grand Palace
and Cascade

The panorama of the Grand Cascade is full of solemnity and grandeur. The diversity of silvery jets, the glitter of the gilded sculpture, Samson's powerful column of water, and the clear-cut architectural forms create a sensation of a joyous holiday. The Grand Cascade is a sort of a pedestal of the Grand Palace and links it with the sea by the straight line of canal. Various arts—architecture, sculpture and fountain and landscape design—have been combined to make this masterpiece, the Grand Cascade.

The idea of artistic decoration of the Grand Cascade dates back to the early 18th century. Its purpose was to glorify the triumphant victory of Russia, which had received an exit to the Baltic Sea and had become one of the powerful countries of Europe.

This idea is repeatedly expressed in an allegorical form in the sculptural decoration of the cascade. More than thirty bronze gilded statues of gods and heroes of antiquity, and twenty-nine bas-reliefs on mythological subjects on the façades of the cascade staircases deal with this theme in one form or another. The general theme of the cascade's sculptural decoration includes three components: the extolling of Russia's triumphant victory in its contest with Sweden during the Northern War, glorification of Russia, prosperous and powerful and mistress of the seas, and satire of the vanquished enemy. The victor country is represented as Perseus who cut off the head of the terrible monster Gorgon Medusa and saved Andromeda. The allegory is clear enough: Perseus is Russia which defeated Sweden and liberated the old Russian lands from foreign domination. The country's inexhaustible wealth is personified in Ceres, the Roman

39

Building under Coat of Arms
of the Grand Palace. 1750—51
Architect B. Rastrelli.
The cupola is decorated
with a rotating weather vane
shaped as a three-headed
eagle with extended wings,
an orb and a scepter in its
claws. The eagle expresses
the idea of the triumph
and greatness of Russia.

goddess of fertility; its sway over the sea in the Tritons, the rulers of waters, and in Galatea symbolizing the calm sea. The leading theme in the allegorical contents of the sculpture of the Grand Cascade was satire of the Swedish usurpers and Charles XII. Thus is interpreted the meaning of the image of Actaeon, a huntsman of a Greek myth, who dared to do what was forbidden by looking at the goddess Diana when she was bathing. The impudent huntsman was exemplarily punished: Diana turned him into a stag and he was torn to pieces by his own hounds. This ancient myth was rightly seen as containing a hint at concrete historical events: the presumptuous Sweden encroached on the sea shores of the powerful Russia and was consequently deservedly punished, betrayed by its own allies.

The Grand Cascade sculpture as a whole is thematically connected with cultural and historical events that were taking place in the Russian state in the Peter I epoch. Turbulent streams of the Volkhov and the Neva Fountains are seething at the foot of the cascade staircases. They derive their names from the allegorical figures of the rivers adorning the fountains, a reminder that the subjugation of the waters in the early 18th century was marked, in part, by the construction of the Ladoga Canal, which helped

...With the Russian powerful hand
The streams of the Volkhóv to ally with the Neva.

The rhythmical movement of the cascade staircases is subordinated to the compositional and ideological center of the whole grandiose fountain complex—the sculpture group of "the Russian Samson who gloriously mangled the roaring Swedish lion". The three-meters-high statue, representing the victorious Russia as the biblical hero, stands on a pedestal resembling a rock and is surrounded with eight jets spouting water from the mouths of bronze gilded dolphins. Above them, shooting out of the mouth of the vanquished lion, rises a 20-meters-high water column that enshrouds Samson's athletic figure in a cloud of sparkling water drops.

Here, in the very heart of the entire ensemble of the Lower Park, the allegory of the sculptural group *Samson Tearing Apart the Lion's Jaws* acquires a special significance. The monument was erected in 1735 to commemorate the 25th anniversary of the battle of Poltava, which decided the outcome of the Northern War in favor of Russia. Its

Vase shaped as an urn,
on the balustrade
of Big Grotto, Grand Cascade
1800
Gilded bronze
Copy from antique original
(2nd century B.C.)

creator was Carlo Rastrelli, the father of the celebrated architect. The famous battle took place on June 27, 1709, the day of St Samson, who was regarded as the "celestial" patron of the Russian warriors, and Sweden's state emblem includes a lion. The sculptural monument thus consummated the idea behind the creation of the Peterhof residence—the glorification of Russia's triumph over a formidable enemy. The dominant position of the Samson Fountain as the focus of the whole composition, besides the height of the jet and its power, is emphasized by yet another noteworthy effect: when the Petrodvorets fountains are turned on, water appears in the lion's open mouth soon to become a 20-meters-high column, but no signs of life are shown yet by the Triton Fountains on the upper terrace of the cascade and the *Sirens* and *Naiads* on the edge of the pool. And only when the Samson jet reaches its highest point, symbolically showing the outcome of the combat, wide arches of water spurt from the shells into which the sea deities are blowing: the rulers of the waters proclaim glory to the hero who has overcome his enemy.

The Grand Cascade presents a striking example of a synthesis of arts: its fountains indeed reveal a close interconnection of all imitative art methods. The architectural solution of the cascade determines the composition of the main ensemble of the park. The three staircases of the cascade are linked by a grotto, its façade having five tall arches with mascarons on the keystones. There is a staircase on the right and on the left of the grotto, each of the seven figured steps of the side cascades decorated with bas-reliefs and brackets. The regular and solemn rhythm of the stairs is accentuated by alternating bronze gilded statues and decorative vases with gilded bronze ornaments. The Samson Fountain stands in a deep semicircular pool merging with the sea canal. On the granite edge of the pool are the *Sirens* and *Naiads* sculpture groups.

Most diverse use in the Grand Cascade is made of streams and spray of water. The main element here is the 20-meters-high water column of the Samson Fountain. As many as 142 jets playing over 64 fountains of the cascade, merging and crossing, make a graceful design completing the architectural features of this monumental structure. Water is used as an active component of the work of art, it is included in the composition of many statues. The movement of water emphasizes dynamism of the sculptures

42

presenting the "victorious images of Russia's glory". Water flows over the staircases in smooth quiet streams, making the spectator follow it with his eyes to the main group expressing the principal idea of the ensemble. The rhythmical distribution of sculpture is in harmony with the location on each step of the side cascade staircases of two strictly vertical jets. The sirens' and naiads' shells throw up silvery water spouts falling in pearl-like drops at the foot of Samson's rock. On the platform in front of the grotto there is the Basket Fountain, the last element of the cascade created in the second half of the 19th century by architect Nikolai Benois. Twenty-four jets interlace above a large tufa ring, forming a delicate pattern, while in the center nine jets rise like sparkling flowers made of water. Water from the Basket flows over the central cascade of three steps into the deep semicircular pool. The Basket Fountain with its abundance of water splendidly completes the enchanting water composition. Water falling from the cascade stairs comes from vertical springs and two fountain-shells on the upper stair and flows as though in natural streams from the semicircular tufa pedestals of the Neva and the Volkhov.

The solemn flow of water pouring into the large pool, the canal naturally linked with the sea and the allegorical sculpture sparkling in the sun all emphasize the principal idea—glorification of Russia's naval victories. The importance of sculpture in the composition of the Grand Cascade is exceptionally great. It not only adorns it but also unites its various parts into a single artistic whole, combining with the architecture and the water scheme. The Grand Cascade was erected simultaneously with the main architectural structures of the Lower Park—the Mon Plaisir Palace and the Upper Palace. Originally, however, the cascade's sculpture was made of lead. The sculpture group *Samson Tearing Apart the Lion's Jaws* was created in 1735 from the same undurable material.

The decorative lead sculpture of the Grand Cascade executed by Carlo Rastrelli, François Pascal, Vassoult and Hans Konrad Ossner from drawings of Le Blond, Braunstein, Michetti and Zemtsov fell into decay by the late 18th century. On August 19, 1799 a decree was issued that, "Instead of the statues standing on the cascade in Peterhof... new ones should be cast in bronze under the Academy of Arts, following in

43

*Samson Tearing Apart
the Lion's Jaws
The central sculptural group
and most powerful fountain
of Grand Cascade. Built in
1735 to commemorate the
25th Anniversary of Battle
of Poltava, it signified
the victories of Russian
arms in the Northern War.
Original sculpture
by C. Rastrelli was in 1802
replaced by a gilded
bronze statue cast after
M. Kozlovsky's model.
Plundered in 1941—44,
Samson was remodeled
by V. Simonov in 1947*

*Grand Cascade sculpture
Sculptural decoration of
Grand Cascade including
255 statues and decorative
details is a most valuable
collection of works
of Russian sculptors
in the late 18th and
early 19th centuries:
I. Martos, F. Shchedrin,
F. Shubin, I. Prokofyev,
F. Gordeev, J. D. Rachette,
and others.
The cascade decoration
most impressively elaborates
the patriotic theme
of glorification
of the power
of the Russian state.*

the choice of figures more of the old models as are to be found on the above-mentioned cascade." The decree was preceded by a careful inspection and a circumstantial report by one of the leading Russian sculptors of the time Ivan Martos.

A galaxy of brilliant Russian sculptors of the 18th century took part in the creation of new sculptures for the Grand Cascade. Many statues were copies of antique originals, models for others were made by Fiodor Shchedrin (*Perseus* and *Sirens*), Fedot Shubin (*Pandora*), Ivan Martos (*Actaeon*), Ivan Prokofyev (*Acis*), and others. The sculptural group of the Samson Fountain was cast after a model made by the outstanding Russian sculptor Mikhail Kozlovsky, the author of the monument to Suvorov in the Field of Mars in Leningrad.

The cascade, built in 1714—21, has in the main preserved its original features as a work of art, full of great power and sublimity.

After the liberation of Petrodvorets, when the decision was taken to restore the unique complex, best Soviet sculptors were commissioned to recreate the plundered statues. The rebirth of the Grand Cascade was an event of great political importance.

Restored to life by Leningrad sculptors V.Simonov and N.Mikhailov, *Samson* again stands as previously in the center of the magnificent cascade. The ceremony of unveiling the biggest fountain in the Lower Park, now a monument to Soviet patriotism, was held on September 14, 1947.

In 1948—50 sculptor I.Krestovsky made anew the statue for the Volkhov Fountain. Excellent work was done by sculptors V.Ellonen, who refashioned the Neva, and N.Dydykin, whose model was used to cast anew the *Tritons* sculptural group.

Raised from the ruins by outstanding restorers, the Peterhof Grand Cascade is now not only a triumphal monument to the victories of Russian arms in the Northern War but also a symbol of the Soviet people's victory over nazism in the Great Patriotic War.

Located symmetrically to the Grand Cascade, there are in the western and eastern parts of the Lower Park two more fountain groups of the same type, decorating the natural slope that borders the park from the south. In the eastern part it is the Checkerboard Hill Cascade and in the western the Golden Hill Cascade.

Faun of Florence,
*on the eastern side
of Grand Cascade. 1800
Gilded bronze. Copy from
antique original (1st—2nd
centuries B.C.);
cast by V. Yekimov
Intoxicated with joy,
Faun, patron of woods
and fields, is beating
a timbrel and dancing.*

Amazon, *on the eastern side
of Grand Cascade. 1801
Gilded bronze. Modeled
by F. Gordeev after antique
original (5th—4th)
centuries B.C.); cast
by V. Yekimov.
Image of an Amazon, one of the
mythological female
warriors, was a reminder
of the invincibility
of the Russian army.*

Pandora, a *Grand Cascade
statue by F. Shubin
She is here a charming young
woman fascinated by the
festive jubilation
of the fountains, not yet
venturing to open the box
enclosing all human ills.*

Perseus, *on the eastern side of Grand Cascade. 1800 Gilded bronze Sculptor F. Shchedrin Perseus was a legendary hero who cut off the head of the Gorgon Medusa, whose gaze turned every living thing into stone. Perseus rescued the beautiful Andromeda from a sea monster. In one hand Perseus holds a sword and in the other the head of Medusa, whose face is an image of Swedish king Charles XII. Perseus and his feat were identified in the 18th century with Peter the Great and his victories.*

Callypigian Venus, *on the eastern side of Grand Cascade. 1857 Gilded copper; copy from antique original (3rd century B.C.); J. A. Hamburger workshop*

Geres, *on the eastern side of Grand Cascade. 1801 Gilded bronze. Modeled by F. Gordeev after antique original; Cast by V. Yekimov The statue of Ceres, the goddess of fertility and agriculture, expresses prosperity of the Russian state.*

Faun of Capitolia, *on the eastern side of Grand Cascade. 1800 Gilded bronze. Copy from antique original (2nd century B.C.); cast by V. Yekimov*

Meleager
of the Belvedere,
*on the eastern side
of Grand Cascade. 1800
Gilded bronze. Modeled
by F. Gordeev
after antique original
(4th century B.C.);
cast by V. Yekimov.
In Greek mythology
Meleager was the hero
who slew the monstruous
Calydonian Boar
and liberated his city
from the enemies.
The sculpture
allegorically glorifies
the feat of arms
of the Russian heroes.*

Bacchus and Satyr,
*on the eastern side
of Grand Cascade. 1800
Gilded bronze
Modeled by F. Gordeev
after Michelangelo;
cast by E. Gastecloux.
Bacchus was the god of
wine making; Satyrs, his
companions, were deities
of mountains and woods.*

Pan and Olympus, *sculptural*
group in the arcade of Big
Grotto, Grand Cascade. 1857
Gilded copper
Copy from antique original;
J. A. Hamburger workshop.
In ancient mythology Pan
was the god of the woods;
Olympus was a legendary
shepherd whom Pan taught
to play the reed-pipe.

Sculpture in the arcade
of Big Grotto, Grand Cascade
In the opening
of the balustrade is
a sculptural group
Tritons Blowing Shells. *1801*
Gilded bronze. Sculptor
I. Prokofyev; recreated
by N. Dydykin in 1949

Pandora, *on the western side of Grand Cascade. 1801 Gilded bronze Sculptor F. Shubin. Pandora was created by command from Zeus to punish the human race for the possession of fire stolen for them from the gods by Prometheus. Zeus gave her in marriage to Prometheus's brother, presenting to them as a wedding gift a box enclosing all human ills. Pandora opened the box out of curiosity and let out all ills, only hope remaining in the box.*

Triumph of Amphitrite, *bas-relief on the façade of the fifth eastern step of Grand Cascade. 1721—23 Gilded and painted lead Modeled by F. P. Vassoult, H. K. Ossner and C. Rastrelli after J.-B. Le Blond and J.-F. Braunstein's drawing; recreated by V. Rubanik in 1947 Amphitrite was the daughter of Nereus, a sage old man of the sea, and consort of the powerful ruler of the seas, Poseidon.*

Deianira Abducted by Centaur Nessus, *bas-relief on the façade of the third eastern step of Grand Cascade. 1721—23 Gilded and painted lead Modeled by F. P. Vassoult, H. K. Ossner and C. Rastrelli after J.-B. Le Blond and J.-F. Braunstein's drawing; recreated by V. Bogatyriov in 1947. Centaur Nessus abducted Deianira. Hercules shot an arrow at the Centaur and freed his wife. The bas-relief allegorically depicts the liberation by Peter I of the Baltic lands.*

Samson Tearing Apart
the Lion's Jaws, *Grand
Cascade. 1802*
*In the center of the pool
mythical sea dwellers
are sending silvery jets
to the pedestal of Samson.
All eyes are turned here,
where a 20-meters-high column
of water shoots from
the mouth of the vanquished
beast and enshrouds in
a cloud of iridescent spray
the athletic figure
of "the Russian Samson
who gloriously mangled
the roaring Swedish lion".*

*Pool of Grand Cascade
In the foreground,
the group* Naiad and Triton;
farther off, Sirens *fountain
group. 1805
Gilded bronze
Sculptor F. Shchedrin.
In ancient mythology sirens
inhabited magic islands;
with their singing they
lured seafarers to their
domain, from where they
never returned.*

60

The Neva,
*on the eastern side
of Grand Cascade pool. 1805
Gilded bronze. Sculptor
F. Shchedrin; recreated
by V. Ellonen in 1950.
Two figures represent
the Russian rivers Neva and
Volkhov. A young woman
squeezing a snake with her
hand symbolize the Neva.
The Volkhov is a powerful
old man with an oar.
The victories won by Peter I
made possible to build
in the first half of the 18th
century the Ladoga Canal
connecting the Volkhov with
the Neva.*

The Volkhov,
*on the western side
of Grand Cascade pool. 1805
Gilded bronze
Sculptor I. Prokofyev;
recreated by I. Krestovsky
in 1948*

Ganymede, *on the western side of Grand Cascade. 1800 Gilded bronze. Copy from original work by Leochares; cast by E. Gastecloux. In ancient mythology Ganymede was a beautiful boy who was carried off by an eagle to Olympus, where Zeus made him gods' cupbearer.*

Western staircase of Grand Cascade In the foreground, sculptures Actaeon *and* Discobolos

Actaeon. *1801*
Gilded bronze
Sculptor I. Martos.
Actaeon was a mythical
huntsman, who, having
surprised Diana bathing,
was changed by the angered
goddess into a stag
and was torn to pieces

by his own hounds.
In the early 18th century
the myth of Actaeon served
in Russia as an allegory
of the presumptuous Swedish
king Charles XII, fleeing
from his former allies, who
took the side of Russia
after the Battle of Poltava.

The Grand Cascade symphony
of fountains

Germanicus, *on the western side of Grand Cascade. 1801 Gilded bronze. Copy from original work by Cleomenes; cast by V. Yekimov. Germanicus was a celebrated Roman general of the 1st century A.D., victor over German tribes.*

Discobolos, *on the western side of Grand Cascade. 1800 Gilded bronze. Copy from antique original (school of Alcamenes); cast by V. Yekimov*

View of the Sea Canal, ▶ Lower Park

Big Parterre

Voronikhin Colonnades

In the Lower Park there are several fountain ensembles harmoniously combining diverse fountains and decorating various sections of its layout. Such ensembles include the Big Flower-Beds, the square at the foot of the Checkerboard Hill, the Mon Plaisir Garden and others. At the foot of the Grand Cascade is the so-called Big Flower-Bed consisting of two symmetrical parts and concluded with Voronikhin Colonnades.

The Voronikhin Colonnades is a unique work of art combining fountains and architecture in the literal sense of the word, ornamental water display with park pavilions.

One of the peculiarities of formal garden planning is the use of various pieces of architecture, most often made of trellises, to hide unwanted, less effective points of view and to direct the spectator's eyes where the impression will be the greatest. Thus, accentuating the splendid perspective of the sea canal and enhancing the idea of direct connection of the Grand Palace with the sea, two wooden galleries were built back in the first quarter of the 18th century on the site of the present marble colonnades.

In the late 18th century the wooden galleries were pulled down and in 1803, Andrei Voronikhin, the most distinguished Russian architect of the period, built in their place rectangular colonnades of twin columns ending on the canal side with pavilions with high cupolas. A low jet of water rises in the center of each gilded cupola, the water flowing over the cupola and then falling in sheets along the windows into a semicircular basin on the ground. Fountains in the form of graceful gilded vases with spouts in the center also stand on the flat lead roofs of the colonnades. These architectural

Ensemble of the central part
of Lower Park
Grand Palace
Terrace Fountains
In the foreground, Big
Flower-Beds and the Italian
Fountain, or the Bowl
1721—22
Designed by N. Michetti;
fountain constructors,
the Barattini brothers

View of Grand Cascade
and the Sea Canal
from the upper terrace
Statues along the cascade
staircases are a unique
parade of over thirty
allegorical images
glorifying the military
victories of Peter I,
the power and prosperity
of Russia: the bellicose
Perseus with the head
of Gorgon Medusa he had cut
off; the graceful, light as
air Galatea, goddess of the
calm sea; the disgraced
and fleeing Actaeon.

decorations turned into original fountain complexes naturally merges with the central composition. Voronikhin's success was recognized by his being awarded the title of architect, and the colonnades have since been known as Voronikhin's. In the 1850s, the Voronikhin Colonnades were faced with color marble after A.Stakenschneider's design.

Damaged during 1941—44, the Colonnades were fully restored in 1966. Their porches, as in the 19th century, are adorned with granite lions hewn after a model of I.Prokofyev. The western and eastern aparts of the parterre are set off with fountains called Bowl Fountains—because of their architectural decor. In the 19th century the figured bowls skillfully made in marble at the Peterhof Lapidary Works replaced the original wooden ones. The edges of the round basin were renewed at the same time. These fountains were designed in the early 18th century by N.Michetti and their waterworks by the Italian Barattini and a Frenchman, Paul Sualem. Hence the often used names of the fountains—Italian and French.

The powerful jets gushing from the depth of the marble vases sparkling in the sun are on the same level as the Samson water column, forming an integral part of the general splendor of the complex.

In the corners of the parterre marble bowls adorned with an ornament and lion's masks rise above semicircular marble benches. These are the Nymph and Danaid Fountains designed by Stakenschneider. There are a typical example of fountains in the mid-19th century, when water was used not as an architectural element but as a decoration helping more vividly to relate the story contained in the sculptures—in this case of the goddess of watersprings, Nymph, and of Danaid, who is doomed to be eternally filling a bottomless vessel. The bronze and copper statues are replicas of the antique original (*Nymph*) and the work of the German sculptor Christian Rauch (*Danaid*).

These two fountains in the corners of the parterre gracefully complete the composition of the Big Flower-Bed in the north.

In the south, on the steps of the natural slope, as though continuing the sumptuous and majestic scene of the Grand Cascade, are situated ten original fountain compositions. They are the Terrace Fountains. On the middle step low jets of water rise over round

marble basins—five from each side of the Grand Cascade. Water from them flows through a bronze mascaron on to a small four-step cascade and from there into a chute common for all the five fountains, decorated with a marble edge of a complex outline. On the lower terrace of the slope five jets rise on each side of the basin-chute. In 1800, the Terrace Fountains were built by architect Franz Brouer in Pudost stone and in 1854 were faced with marble. After restoration they were opened in 1946.

By the end of the 18th century the main fountain decoration of the Lower Park was thus completed. Fountains by the Sea Canal were erected considerably earlier. The initial plan was to adorn it with the so-called "niche" fountains, that is, ones placed in trellis niches, which were to be on the subjects of Aesop's fables. Four wooden groups were installed by 1724 already but, soon falling into decay, were removed. One of the groups, repeated in metal (in 1725), is still there. Three figures of ducks and the figure of a dog, named Favorite, are turning round and round with the help of a water wheel in the middle of a round basin. The ducks' open beaks and the open mouth of the dog spray water. The fountain is called the Favorite and enacts Aesop's fable *The Dog and the Ducks*. The edifying intent is accentuated by a special tablet with the content of the fable written on it: "A doggie was chasing ducks in water; then the ducks told her this: your pains are in vain, you have the power to chase us but have no power to catch us." So the remaining "niche" fountain is a reminder of the initial plan of decorating the canal.

In 1735 M.Zemtsov moved the fountains nearer to the edge of the canal, designing for them new basins of Pudost stone in the form of flower baskets with two grips. Eight of the 22 basins have retained the form of the 1735 baskets, while the others were in the mid-19th century replaced with marble rings. Water from the 22 fountains in the Fountains Alley runs into the canal through the openings in the gilded mascarons fixed on its walls. Thus artistically interconnected "playing water" decorates the complex of the central part of the Lower Park in front of the Peterhof Grand Palace.

Lion, *by the western Voronikhin Colonnade. 1802 Granite. Sculptor I. Prokofyev*

Voronikhin Colonnades (eastern and western). 1800—3 The two marble colonnades closing the composition of parterres in front of the Grand Cascade were built according to the drawings of outstanding Russian architect

A. Voronikhin. Eight granite lions cut after I. Prokofyev's models lay at the entrances to the galleries on the sides of the stairs. During 1941—44, marble facing of Voronikhin Colonnades was considerably damaged. Restoration work was done in 1961—65 according to A. Gessen's design. Gilded cupolas and bowl-shaped fountains on the colonnades were restored at the same time.

78

*Danaid Fountain,
on the eastern parterre
in front of Grand
Cascade. 1853
Designed
by A. Stakenschneider
Danaid
Gilded bronze. Modeled
by I. Vitali after
Ch. Rauch.
Danaid was a daughter
of mythological king
Danaus; for the murder
of her husband she was
condemned to fill with
water a bottomless
vessel.*

Nymph Fountain,
on the western parterre
near Grand Cascade.
1853
Designed
by A. Stakenschneider
Nymph
Gilded copper. Copy
from antique original
(3rd century B.C.)
In Greek mythology
Nymph was goddess
of springs.

*Eve Fountain,
on Marly Alley. 1726
Designed by N. Michetti
Compositional center
of the western part
of Lower Park*

Adam and Eve Fountains

Two similar fountains close the perspectives of the transverse alleys leading from the Grand Cascade to the Hermitage and Mon Plaisir. In the middle of octahedral basins stand marble statues surrounded with a garland of 16 water-sprays, *Adam* in the eastern part and *Eve* in the western. Each structure closes the perspective of eight alleys radially converging on the place where the sculpture stands. The fountains themselves are placed strictly symmetrical to the Sea Canal. The Adam Fountain is one of the first fountains in the Lower Park. The Eve Fountain is several years younger, but their location and the planning of the sections where they stand show strict observance by the architects of the Lower Park of the principles of formal garden layout and the unity of the scheme. The marble statues modeled by Giovanni Bonazza after Antonio Ricci's originals in Venice, brought to Russia in 1717, were, in the opinion of the contemporaries, so beautiful that even "in the glorious Versailles few such can be found". The Adam Fountain, however, was opened only in 1722 and Eve in 1726. The two fountains were designed by N.Michetti.

The statue of the mythical first man of the earth is taken as personifying Peter the Great, for just as Adam started the human race, Peter "brought the Russians from non-existence to existence". This opinion, widespread in 19th century literature, is confirmed by the story of creation of the Eve Fountain. It was built after the death of Peter, when his wife Catherine I "graciously indicated where to put up Eve's fountain". The empress, apparently supporting the already current view of Peter I as of the "great transformer of Russia", wanted to emphasize her own participation in the reforms, symbolically portraying herself as Eve, the "first" woman on the earth. The fountains were restored in 1949.

Adam Fountain,
on Marly Alley. 1722
Designed by N. Michetti
Compositional center
of the eastern part
of Lower Park
Adam. 1718
Marble. Free copy
by G. Bonazza after A. Ricci

Eve. 1718
Marble. Free copy
by G. Bonazza after A. Ricci

Mon Plaisir Palace,
southern façade
Peter I's seaside palace
designed by J.-F. Braunstein,
J.-B. Le Blond and
N. Michetti was built
in 1714—23;
was considerably damaged
during 1941—44

Ensemble of the Western Part of Lower Park

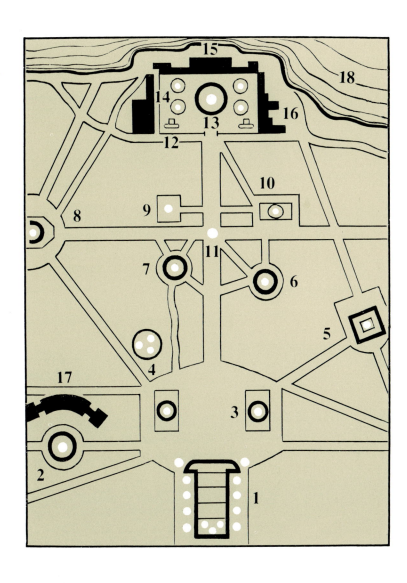

1 Checkerboard Hill
   Cascade
2 Triton Fountain
3 Roman Fountains
4 Little Fir Fountains
5 Pyramid Fountain
6 Chinese Parasol Fountain
7 Oaklet Fountain
8 Adam Fountain
9 Western Aviary
10 Sun Fountain
11 Monument to Peter I
12 Jester Fountains
13 Sheaf Fountain
14 Cloche Fountains
15 Mon Plaisir
16 Chinese Garden
17 Conservatory
18 Gulf of Finland

Mon Plaisir Garden
Chinese Garden
Jester Fountains
Sun Fountain

The Mon Plaisir Garden was created as a miniature formal garden. Five fountains in the centers of the separate sections of this small garden constitute its water decoration.

Two alleys crossing at right angles divide the square area of the Mon Plaisir Garden into four small sections. Twenty-five jets of the Sheaf Fountain play in the middle of the garden. The centers of the small squares are decorated with the Cloche Fountains, so called because the water softly running down the figured pedestals of the four gilded bronze statues forms transparent round "bells", or *cloches*.

The fountains were constructed by a special order: "In Mon Plaisir, in the middle of the garden, to put up at the crossing Fountain No 1; and to make for the four gilded statues round copper turned pedestals, not too thick, to place them after gilding and to supply with water so that it should run from under the latter to the ground smoothly like glass".

The order is dated by the year 1721 and in 1723 all the fountains were ready. The central fountain derives its name from its pattern: the scattering spray of the jets resemble a sheaf of ripe wheat ears shedding its grain. 19th century books mention also another name of the fountain, the Crown. In the same century the original pattern of the jets was changed, and the sculptured tufa decoration had the form of a crown. In the post-war years the various complexes in the Lower Park were restored in such a way that wherever possible they might resume their 18th century appearance. The central fountain of the Mon Plaisir has thus acquired its original form.

The sculpture on the pedestals of the Cloche Fountains was cast in bronze and gilded in 1817 after models of I.Martos. It replaced the previous disfigured lead statues. On the

89

Chinese Garden. 1860
Designed by E. Hahn
Shell Fountain with
sculptural group
Cupid and Psyche
First half of the 19th century
Marble. Copy from
A. Canova's model
after antique original
(2nd century B.C.)

pedestals reproduced by sculptor A.Troupiansky again stand the sculptures *Satyr with Goat* and *Apollino*, copies from antique originals, *Psyche* copying the statue of Canova, and *Bacchus* created after Sansovino's original. In the east, the Mon Plaisir Bath building and the Assembly Hall with the kitchens are adjoined by the coastal Chinese Garden. Designed by Eduard Hahn in the landscape style, it was laid out in 1860.

Observing the principles of Japanese and Chinese garden-making, the designer tried to create within a small area a diversity of scenery. The whimsical paths, flower-beds, a winding rivulet with an arched little bridge, marble statues and shady trees make it an extremely cozy nook.

An artificial mound diversifies the terrain of the garden; the mount has in it a grotto decorated with tufa. A stream flows from the grotto along the edges of two marble shells, which have given the name to the fountain, Shell. A high jet shoots from the middle of a small islet. The five fountains of the Mon Plaisir Garden close the perspective of the alley running from the Checkerboard Hill Cascade, and on the parterre flower-beds in front of the cascade, symmetrically to it, there are two fountains called Roman.

Of the "jester" fountains still existing in the Lower Park the first to be built were the two benches in the Mon Plaisir Garden. They were placed opposite the palace pleasure houses. The benches made of trellises and the graveled ground in front of them were in the 18th century covered with a trellis bower. Covered green galleries led there from to the side wings of Mon Plaisir. The peculiarity of the fountains is that they are turned on unexpectedly and shower with water unsuspecting visitors of Peterhof who might want to take a rest in the picturesque Mon Plaisir Garden.

Two more jester fountains appeared in the Lower Park in the late 18th and the early 19th centuries. In 1803, a metal tree, Oaklet, skillfully made according to a drawing of C.Rastrelli, was removed from Upper to Lower Park. Each one of the tree's branches and the metal brightly coloured tulips surrounding it end with a tube with water shooting from it. A visitor, admiring the beautiful decoration of the fountain, does not notice that water starts shooting from behind the garden benches and suddenly pours over him.

The Oaklet was destroyed during the war. Fountain-making specialists A.Lavrentyev

and A.Smirnov, using as a model one twig found when the debris was being cleared, recreated the original fountain. Also recreated was the Chinese Parasol Fountain, initially built after a design of architect F. Brouer in 1796. You can easily step under the parasol but find it impossible to step out when 164 jets send down the parasol a solid sheet of water. Not far from the Oaklet, there are the Little Fir Fountains. The three small metal trees were created in 1784. Their trunks are made of steel pipes chased to look like natural bark and the branches of brass, while the needles are tin colored green. From afar the fir-trees look like real ones and only close by one can see that they are covered with a thin veil of water spurting out of the twigs.

The jester fountains of the Lower Park are unique. Similar trick effects were used in Versailles and other parks but today they have remained only in Petrodvorets. They are especially admired by youthful visitors of the Peterhof ensemble. Indeed, the builders made the fountain jets take most fantastic and unexpected forms. Thus, one of the sections of the park is adorned with a fountain named the Sun.

*Bath Building of Mon Plaisir
Palace. 1866
Designed by E. Hahn
View from the palace façade
and the Chinese Garden*

*Sun Fountain. 1774—75
Designed by Yu. Felten
and I. Yakovlev.
A bronze revolving pole
terminates in gilded disks,
from which jets of water
shoot like sun rays*

In the 1770s in the section called Ménagerie, architects Yu. Felten and I. Yakovlev transformed the former pond, where rare waterfowl were kept, into the royal bath house. The pond was surrounded with high walls and a fountain was installed in the middle of it. Its purpose was to shower the bathers. Two gilded bronze disks with holes on the outer edge of each were fastened to a tall pole originally decorated with round glass lampions silvered from inside and sparkling in the sun. The round pedestal decorated with tufa and 16 fountains in the form of dolphins concealed a water wheel which made the pole turn round. The gilded disks glittered in the sun and the shooting jets resembled rays. Hence the name—the Sun. In 1925 the walls of the bath house were torn down and the fountain was included in the system of decorative elements of the Lower Park.

Restored in 1956, the fountain represents an interesting sample of a mechanical fountain and is invariably popular with the visitors of Peterhof, just as the famous jester fountains.

Psyche, *statue*
in Mon Plaisir Alley. 1830s
Marble. Copy from
A. Canova's work

Western aviary. 1721—22
Wooden domed aviary faced
with tufa and shells,
the interior still remaining
ornamental and topical
painting dealing with the
myth of Diana and Actaeon,
executed by L. Caravaque

Roman Fountains

Architectural solution of the Roman fountains is simple: two octagons are placed on one another and decorated with slabs of white, grey and pink marble and bronze gilded details—mascarons, garlands and wreaths. The lower octagon is larger than the upper and each of them represents a sort of a sculptural support for water. From the upper vase rise five jets, with water falling over the crown of the upper and then the lower bowl in a thin yarn.

The name of the fountains, Roman, is due to the fact that they resemble the ones near the St Peter's Cathedral in Rome.

The Roman Fountains were created in 1739 by architects I. Blank and I. Davydov, and in 1763 were reconstructed by B. Rastrelli. At the end of the 18th century they were faced with coloured marble and had bronze ornaments added to them. Restoration of the fountains was completed in 1954.

Pluto and Pomona,
at Checkerboard Hill Cascade
Early 18th century
Marble
Work of Italian sculptors.
In ancient mythology Pluto
was the god of the under-
world and wealth. With his
left hand he holds an over-
turned horn of plenty, with
money, fruit and flowers
pouring out of it; on his
right, the three-headed dog,
Cerberus, which guarded the
entrance to Hades. Pomona
was the goddess of autumnal
abundance of fruit. In her
right hand she holds a horn
of plenty filled with fruit
and flowers.

Checkerboard Hill Cascade

Conservatory

The Checkerboard Hill Cascade is the focal fountain structure in the eastern part of the Lower Park, made up of four drain-slopes decorated with tufa stone and two grottos, the upper and the lower. The upper grotto is closed with a heavy door, with two winged dragons sprawling in front of it as though guarding the entrance to a wonderland.

Water streams from the dragons' mouths, falling in a transparent veil into a small semicircular basin at the foot of the ridge in front of the lower grotto. Black and white squares show through the water current. The oil-painted steps of the cascade resemble checkerboards. From the upper terrace one can descend along the tufa base by two staircases, eastern and western. On the outside of each of them are placed five marble sculptures. Put up on high pedestals of gray stone, they make an integral part of the cascade decoration.

Designed by Michetti, the construction of the cascade was started in 1721, following Peter I's order "to make a marble cascade with a small grotto and a wild hill". The structure was then called the "Ruins Cascade": in the postscript to his order the tsar bade to erect on the hill a ruined fortress tower symbolizing the capture of a Swedish fortress.

At the end of the 1730s, however, architect M.Zemtsov, instructed to reconstruct the structure, made the four drain-slopes, and in front of the upper grotto sculptor H. K. Ossner put three woodcarved figures of dragons from drawings of I.Davydov and I.Blank and painted with oil-paint. Hence the second name of the cascade, the Dragon Hill, while its present name was acquired in the middle of the 18th century, when the drainstairs began to be painted with black and white squares.

◄

Checkerboard Hill Cascade is the most important fountain composition of the eastern part of Lower Park. Initially the cascade, whose construction was started in 1721, was to be decorated as ruins of a Swedish fortress, which determined its early name, Ruins. In the late 1730s it was decorated anew by I. Davydov and I. Blank:

three woodpainted dragons made by H. K. Ossner were installed, and the cascade began to be called Dragon Hill, and from 1769, when the drain-slopes were painted in black and white squares, Checkerboard Hill. Its marble statues are an important collection of decorative park sculpture of the 18th century.

Jupiter, at Checkerboard Hill Cascade. Early 18th century Marble. Work of Italian sculptor Jupiter, the ruler of the universe, has the globe as a support for his foot; on his right side is an eagle with extended wings. This statue was an allegory of Russia's greatness.

The appearance of the Checkerboard Hill Cascade changed somewhat in the mid-19th century: Nikolai Benois replaced the wooden figures by leaden, arranging them frontally in one row. They were plundered by the nazis, and in their place now stand bronze ones remodeled by sculptor A.Gurzhy according to the designs and drawings of the 18th century.

The Checkerboard Hill marble statues are a very rare collection of decorative park sculpture of the 18th century. Especially expressive are the figures of Pomona, goddess of autumnal abundance, of Adonis, god of the reviving and dying nature, and Pluto, god of the underworld. The nazis could not find the buried sculpture, and now the marble statues have taken their former places. The cascade has been restored and in all its magnificence delights the visitors of Petrodvorets.

Yet another interesting fountain among those conceived in the first quarter of the 18th century is Triton, or Conservatory Fountain, as it is called by the place where it is situated.

In the center of the Conservatory Garden, on the approaches to the Grand Cascade from the east, a bronze group *Triton Tearing Apart the Jaws of a Sea Monster*, similar in its idea to Samson, stands in a round basin. Initially the sculpture was leaden, it was created by sculptor C.Rastrelli after a design of T.Usov. At the end of the 18th century already, during his inspection tour to Peterhof, Martos mentioned its state of extreme decay and the necessity of replacement. Only in 1876, however, a new sculptural group, *Triton with Crocodile*, was made by galvanoplastic method after drawings and models of David Jensen. The sculptural group was plundered during 1941—44. At the present time the sculptural decoration of the fountain has been reproduced, according to 18th century designs and drawings, by sculptor A.Gurzhy. Of invaluable aid in such work are the pictures in the albums of P.Saint-Hilaire, A.Bazhenov and others to be found in the Peterhof archives. Water decoration of the Triton Fountain consists of five jets—the central powerful jet snooting from the mouth of the monster and four low ones spouting from the open mouths of bronze tortoises. The fountain complements the ornamentation of the Conservatory complex and unites it with the other sections of the Lower Park.

Fountain figures of winged
dragons at Checkerboard Hill
Cascade. 1739
Painted bronze. Sculptors
I. Blank, I. Davydov and
H. K. Ossner; recreated
by A. Gurzhy in 1952
after 18th century drawings

Big Conservatory Pavilion.
1722—24
Designed by J.-F. Braunstein
During 1941—44 the building
was burnt down by the
invaders. The Conservatory
was restored after V. Savkov's
design in 1954.
Big Conservatory is one
of the most interesting
monuments of 18th century
garden architecture. From the
central two-storied
building run gently curving
galleries ending in jutties.
Light balustrade adorn
the façades of the building.

Triton (Conservatory)
Fountain. 1726
In the center of the
orchard, in front of the
southern façade of Big
Conservatory, there is
a fountain (designed
by T. Usov) with the sculptural
group Triton Tearing Apart
the Jaws of Sea Monster (1726),
work of C. Rastrelli.
Stolen in 1941—44,
Triton was remodeled
in bronze by A. Gurzhy in 1956

In the eastern part of the park, the section called Pyramid Garden is decorated with one of the most beautiful fountains, Pyramid. Water dominates in the architectural solution of this water obelisk, which is visible from afar; without the foaming and glittering streams it is dead and meaningless. The Pyramid Fountain amazes by its decorative peculiarities. A foamy mass of water in the form of a regular pyramid made by 505 jets of various height rises in the middle of a square basin on a granite pedestal with marble steps, surrounded by a graceful balustrade with vases. The sparkling water monolith contrasts with the dense greenery of the surrounding trees and the dark water of the Gulf of Finland, a view of which opens in the perspective of the alley running north. The fountain was the work of N.Michetti and M.Zemtsov (1724). The design of its ingenious water supplying device, making possible to regulate the height of the jets and to create a geometrically precise seven-step pyramid, was made by the talented French hydraulic engineer Paul Sualem. The fountain was restored in 1953.

Ensemble of the Eastern Part of Lower Park

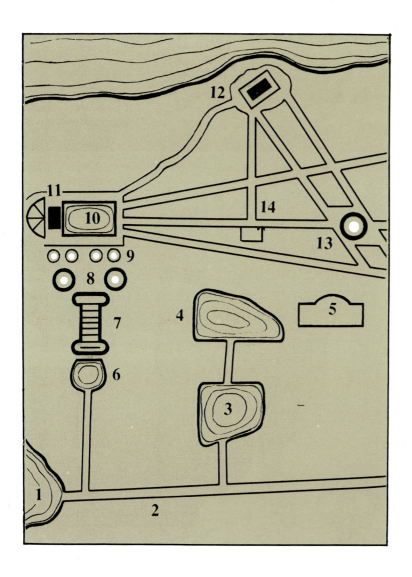

1 English Pond
2 Upper Garden canal
3 Dry Pond
4 Eve Basin
5 Sand Pond
6 Marly Pond
7 Golden Hill Cascade
8 Ménagerie Fountains
9 Triton, or Cloche Fountains
10 Marly Pond
11 Marly Palace
12 Hermitage Pavilion
13 Eve Fountain
14 Lion Cascade

Golden Hill Cascade
Andromeda
Early 18th century
Marble. Sculptor P. Baratta.
Andromeda is chained
to a rock. Her long hair is
hanging down her back. On her
right is the head of a sea monster.

Marly Cascade Fountains

Yet another cascade, Golden Hill, is situated symmetrically with the Checkerboard Hill Cascade, on the other side of the canal, in the western part of the Lower Park. The construction of the Marly Cascade (Golden Hill) was started by instructions from Peter I, the idea having been prompted to him by a similar structure in the Park Marly near Paris.

The cascades of that park produced a very strong impression on Peter and he ordered that "the great cascade, which is opposite the pond, should be in everything proportionate to the Marly Cascade opposite the royal palace". But the peculiarities of natural conditions and the creative distinctiveness of the Russian architects made possible to create an original, full of harmony ensemble the western part of the Lower Park.

The beginning of construction of Golden Hill is dated by 1721, when Michetti made the design for adorning the natural slope with a majestic 22-step cascade staircase, and Carlo Rastrelli was given instructions to make a group for it depicting "the story of Hercules, who is fighting a seven-headed serpent called Hydra...." The work was in the main completed by 1726, but the sculptural group was never made.

Its present appearance the cascade acquired in the 1730s. The one who worked at that time in Peterhof most intensively was the famous architect M.Zemtsov. He reconstructed the Marly Cascade, adding to it marble and gilded statues, and the steps of the cascade staircase were by his instruction faced with gilded copper plates. Hence the present name of the cascade, Golden Hill. A considerable part of the collection of marble sculptures appeared here later: they replaced the statues put up according to M.Zemtsov's design only in the mid-19th century.

Complex restoration of the Golden Hill cascade has now been completed. Its constructive elements have been remade. The wooden staircases with balustrades have been replaced by stone. The marble facing of the drain stairs has been restored. From the three gilded mascarons of sea monsters on the upper wall of the cascade water flows over the 22 marble stairs with their fronts faced with gilded copper plates.

The marble statues flanking the cascade, the gilded steps and the granite staircases whose landings offer a view of the sea, the Marly Palace and the Ménagerie Fountains give the whole structure a scope and a magnitude.

Six fountains decorate the parterre at the Golden Hill Cascade. The jets of the so-called Ménagerie Fountains, with a diameter of 30 cm, creating the impression of abundance of water and great power, rise in two round basins symmetrically to the cascade. The fountains were erected in 1722—25, and their name derives from the French word "ménager" to save, to economize. The fountains' exuberance is deceptive, their jets are empty inside. Nevertheless their effect is magnificent and was formerly enhanced by gilded hollow balls playing on the tops of the water pillars, now no longer there.

The Golden Hill ensemble is supplemented with four Triton-Cloche Fountains. Baby tritons hold over their heads bowls with edges turned down. Water flows on to the bowl from a pipe with a cap fixed to it, which makes water fall in the form of a transparent veil. The present bronze figures of tritons have replaced the sculpture cast back in 1721, in the year of creation of the fountains, which was plundered by the nazis.

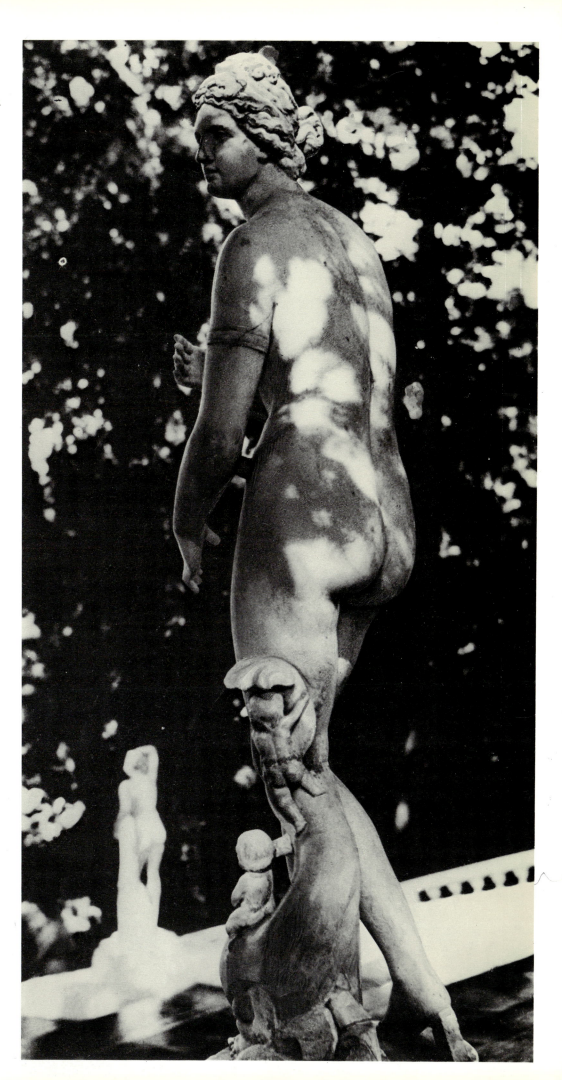

Marly Palace,
or Minor Palace. 1721—23
Designed by J.-F. Braunstein.
The name derives
from the residence
of the French king,
Louis XIV, near Paris.

Golden Hill Cascade
Venus de' Medici
Late 18th century
Marble. Copy from antique
original by Timarch
and Kephisodotes
(3rd century B.C.)
The goddess of beauty is
slightly bending forward,
with a dolphin at her feet.

Golden Hill Cascade
Neptune. *Early 18th century*
Marble. Sculptor A. Tarsia.
In ancient mythology
Neptune was the god of the
sea. With his right hand he
touches the dolphin's tail
and with his left holds
the drapery.

Golden Hill Cascade
Flora. *18th century*
Marble. Sculptor G. Zorzoni

Triton, or Cloche Fountain
Early 18th century
Designed by J.-F. Braunstein;
was destroyed during 1941—44;
recreated in 1955

Big Ménagerie Fountain
1724
Designed by N. Michetti

Afterword

Petrodvorets has on its grounds, besides regular, several landscape parks, occupying an area of over 1,000 hectares with many palatial buildings, pavilions and minor structures.

But all this was not up to the artistic perfection, to the amazing unity of the idea and its realization which is characteristic of the complex of the Lower and the Upper Parks. The palaces, parks and fountains of Peterhof are monuments of an important period, the time of great constructive changes which made Russia one of the leading states of the world, heightening its national self-consciousness and opening up new ways of economic and cultural progress. In this sense Peterhof-Petrodvorets can be called a monument of Russian glory. One of the most striking peculiarities of its formal palace-and-park ensemble consists in its extremely impressive, organic synthesis of various types of artistic activity—architecture, sculpture, and fountain and garden making.

Anyone who has at least once been its visitor will always cherish the memory of the "old as its legends and ever youthful Peterhof".

List of Plates

In the album 18th century Russian engravings
and details from them are reproduced.
Ensemble of the western part of Lower
Park is represented according to archive
records.

INDEX

Фонтаны
Петродворца
The Fountains
of Petrodvorets
near Leningrad

Издательство
«Советский художник»
Москва. 1980

Изд. № 3-407